Table of Contents

Rourke Educational Media

A Division of Carson Dellosa Education

rourkeeducationalmedia.com

Can you find these words?

gifts

nativity

Santa

tree

We Celebrate Christmas!

Christmas comes in December.

Let’s light the winter night!

Some towns light a Christmas tree.

Let's decorate!

Some families set up a **nativity.**

Let's cook!

Some people bake cookies.

Let’s wait!

Some kids wait for **Santa** Claus.

Let's give!

Gifts bring joy to all.

Did you find these words?

Gifts bring joy to all.

Some families set up a **nativity**.

Some kids wait for **Santa** Claus.

Some towns light a Christmas **tree**.

Photo Glossary

gifts (gifts): Items given as presents.

nativity (nuh-TI-vuh-tee): A scene that shows the birth of Jesus.

Santa (SAN-tuh): A plump man with a white beard and a red suit who delivers presents to children.

tree (tree): A tall plant with branches and bark. A real or fake tree is often decorated for Christmas.

Index

About the Author

Lisa Jackson is a writer from Columbus, Ohio. She likes to ride her bike and collect pennies. Her favorite holiday is the one that is coming up next!

www.rourkeeducationalmedia.com

PHOTO CREDITS: Cover: ©By Yuganov Konstantin; Pg 2, 10, 14, 15 ©inhauscreative; Pg 2, 12, 14, 15 ©Steve Debenport; Pg 2, 4, 14, 15 ©andykazie; Pg 2, 6, 14, 15 ©edimur; Pg 3 ©kajakiki; Pg 9 ©acongar

Edited by: Keli Sipperley
Cover and interior design by: Kathy Walsh

Library of Congress PCN Data
Christmas / Lisa Jackson
(Holidays Around the World)
ISBN 978-1-73160-574-0 (hard cover)(alk. paper)
ISBN 978-1-73160-438-5 (soft cover)
ISBN 978-1-73160-623-5 (e-Book)
ISBN 978-1-73160-675-4 (ePub)
Library of Congress Control Number: 2018967327

Printed in the United States of America,
North Mankato, Minnesota